The Chapel
and
The Nation

Nonconformity and The Local Historian

Michael R. Watts

Published by

The Historical Association

59a Kennington Park Road

London SE11 4JH

About the author

Michael R. Watts is Reader in Modern History at the University of Nottingham and the author of *The Dissenters*, vol i, *From the Reformation to the French Revolution* (Oxford, 1978, 1985); *The Dissenters*, vol ii, *The Expansion of Evangelical Nonconformity, 1791-1859* (Oxford, 1995); and *Religion in Victorian Nottinghamshire: The Religious Census of 1851* (2 vols, Nottingham, 1988). He is now working on a third volume of *The Dissenters* which will cover the second half of the nineteenth and twentieth centuries.

The Historical Association, founded in 1906, brings together people who share an interest in, and love for, the past. It aims to further the study and teaching of history at all levels: teacher and student, amateur and professional. This is one of over 100 publications available at very preferential rates to members.

Membership also includes journals at generous discounts and gives access to courses, conferences, tours and regional and local activities. Full details are available from The Secretary at the address below.

Edited by
Clive H. Knowles

Origination and Layout by
Marco Spinelli

Published by The Historical Association, 59a Kennington Park Rd, London SE11 4JH and printed in Great Britain by Blackmore Press, Longmead, Shaftesbury, Dorset SP7 8PX

ISBN 0 85278-395-7

Front cover illustration shows John Wesley addressing Methodist preachers in City Road Chapel, London. *Wesley's Chapel*

Contents

Introduction:
The Chapel and the Nation   5

Radicals and Puritans,
1532-1660   9

Persecution and Toleration,
1660-1730   14

Unitarians and Evangelicals,
1730-1851   19

Crisis and Conscience,
from 1851   26

References   33

Glossary of Terms used in
Histories of Nonconformity   37

Suggestions for Further
Reading   41

Introduction: The chapel and the nation

The Nonconformist chapel has played a crucial role in the history of the English and Welsh nations. When the great French historian Elie Halévy sought to explain the contrast between the turbulent history of his own country and the peaceful evolution of England in the late eighteenth and nineteenth centuries he found the key in the latter country's Evangelical religious revival, of which the Nonconformist denominations were the chief beneficiaries. The role of the Nonconformists, argued Halévy, was crucial in preserving England from the revolutions that racked so much of Europe in the nineteenth century.

> For all their freedom of theological difference the [Nonconformist] sects agreed among themselves and with the national authorities to impose on the nation a rigorous ethical con-formity and at least an outward respect for the Christian social order.[1]

There are, of course, many other factors which help to explain the divergent histories of England and much of conti-nental Europe: the comparative absence of fear of foreign invasion, the success of parliament in curbing the power of the monarchy, the early development of overseas commerce and of mechanised industry. But there can be no doubt that a major influence distinguishing the history of England from that of her continental neighbours has been the success of Protestant Nonconformity in guaranteeing that England enjoyed religious, and therefore political, pluralism earlier than most other European nations. The

Separatists of Elizabethan and early Stuart England struggled against a persecuting State Church to uphold the principle that religion is essentially a contract between the individual believer and his or her Maker, not a matter of obedience to the magistrate. The Independents and Baptists of the 1640s and 1650s maintained that church membership was a matter of voluntary subscription to a covenant, not of genuflecting before king or bishop. Of the many sectarian churches founded during the Civil Wars and Interregnum some survived the return of Charles II and the Clarendon Code to become the oldest democratic institutions existing in England today. The toleration and pros-perity that followed the overthrow of James II in 1688 sapped the Dissenters' zeal and by the second quarter of the eighteenth century was diminishing their numbers: even at the accession of George I not much more than 6 per cent of the population of England, and less than 6 per cent of the population of Wales, could be counted as Nonconformist. But the Evangelical revival of the late eighteenth and early nineteenth centuries brought a vast increase in the adherents of the Baptists and Congregationalists and ultimately added to them the biggest Nonconformist denomination of all: the Methodists. By 1851 17 per cent of the population of England and a staggering 45 per cent of the population of Wales were worshipping in Nonconformist chapels. A minority of Dissenters, especially Quakers and Unitarians, were prosperous business men who made a distinctive contribution to Britain's industrial expansion. But the overwhelming majority of Baptists, Congregationalists, and Methodists were poor semi-skilled and unskilled workers and their wives, and in the first half of the nineteenth century the chapels of the Evangelical Nonconformists had a far greater attraction for working-class families than had political radicalism, Owenism, or Chartism.

Whether the Nonconformist churches have had a beneficial or a deleterious influence on modern England and Wales is a matter of dispute. The Nonconformist chapel was one of the main agencies in the propagation of 'Victorian values'. The sense of probity, thrift, enterprise, devotion to work, and self-discipline that characterised the English and Welsh nations in the nineteenth and first half of the twentieth centuries owed a very great deal to Nonconformity. The fact that these values were cherished not only by many members of the middle class but also by a substantial section of the working class meant that Dissent played an important part in forging the social harmony that was one of the outstanding features of mid-Victorian society. Politically, too, Dissenters made a distinctive contribution. Nonconformists were the most consistent and reliable element in support of the Victorian and Edwardian Liberal party and by 1906 of 401 Liberal MPs nearly half, 190, were Nonconformists. Dissent brought to the Liberal party a passion for humanitarian reform and social justice that found expression in the reforms of the great Liberal governments of 1905-14. The decline of the Liberal party did not end the distinctive Nonconformist contribution to political life: the passion for social justice was transferred to the Labour party and in 1925 out of 192 Labour MPs 45 had been Nonconformist lay preachers. It was the influence of Nonconformity that helped to prevent the cleavage between Christianity and Socialism that has had so catastrophic an effect on so many continental countries. Many of the social ills from which we now suffer, the decline in personal probity, the increase in crime and corruption, are arguably the result of the rejection of the values inculcated by Dissent.

Alternatively Nonconformity can be seen as having had a damaging effect on the lives of English and Welsh peoples. It can be argued that it preached a particularly narrow and selfish version of Christianity which sought to brand every harmless pleasure from dancing to playing cricket as sin, and which taught that the penalty for such sin was eternal punishment in the fires of hell. Dissent had a particularly baneful influence on the lives of countless thousands of people by persuading them that normal sexual feelings were evil and so condemning them to miserable, guilt-ridden lives. The social and economic consequences of Dissent were equally disastrous because the Nonconformists' narrow brand of religion led them to argue that the root cause of social evils was sin and that their only solution lay in individual conversion and personal morality: Nonconformist individualism strengthened the concept of *laissez-faire* and so frustrated attempts to deal with the fundamental causes of human poverty. By teaching a substantial section of the working class to be patient in the face of suffering and quiescent in the face of injustice Dissent contributed to the social control whereby the upper classes kept the poor in a state of docile subservience. The evil influence of Dissent extended even to foreign affairs. It persuaded public and politicians alike that a sentimental morality should take the place of the pursuit of national interest and so contributed to the decline of British power and influence in the world. It was no coincidence that so many of Britain's leaders in the 1930s came from Dissenting stock: Neville Chamberlain, John Simon, Samuel Hoare. So persistent was the Nonconformist belief that peace could be preserved by moral example rather than by military hardware that, notwithstanding the experiences of the Second World War, Nonconformists and their descendants played a prominent role in the Campaign for Nuclear Disarmament.

Support for these opposing views of Nonconformity, for the defence and for the prosecution, can he found in any decent run of church minute books in any County Record Office and in many a church cupboard. Just because the Nonconformist churches were so democratic, just because the Baptists, Congregationalists, and Quakers had monthly church meetings, just because the Methodists and Quakers had Quarterly Meetings to regulate the affairs of their local areas, we know far more about the life of Dissenters at chapel level than we do about the workings of the Church of England at parish level. Church minute books record details of the admission and dismissal of members, of the election and removal of ministers, of the building and demolition of chapels, of the disciplining of recalcitrant members and the reprimanding of reprobate politicians. There is thus within the easy reach of every local historian a rich storehouse of material to enable him or her to reconstruct the history of his local Baptist, Congregationalist, Methodist, or Quaker community and to make his own distinctive contribution to the history not only of his local chapel but also to that of his nation.

affemble of Brownifts, Separatifts, and Non-Confor-
, as they met together at a private houfe to heare a Sermon of a
brother of theirs neere _Algate_, being a learned _Felt-maker._

ontayning the whole difcourfe of his Expofition, with the man-
ner and forme of his preaching, praying, giving thankes be-
fore and after Dinner and Supper, as it was lately heard
and now difcovered by a brother of theirs who
is turned out of their Society upon fome
difcontent, to be buffeted by Sathan.

Auditors were _Button-makers_, _Tranflaters_, _Weavers_, _Box-makers_,
with divers other holy Brethren and _Sifters._

Printed 1641.

The Brownists were named after Robert Browne, who advocated the setting up of
gathered churches separate from the established Church of England. The
illustration reveals the horror with which many contemporaries regarded lay-
preaching by the lower orders. _The British Library (Thomason Collection)_

Radicals and Puritans, 1532-1660

The local historian will be exceptionally lucky if he can find any evidence of Nonconformist activity in his neighbourhood before 1640. Before that date men and women who deliberately separated themselves from the established Church of England appear in the historical records only when they were dragged before the courts for their disobedience, and this was something that they were obviously anxious to avoid. Under Henry VIII and his daughter Mary I men and women who repudiated official religious dogma were burned at the stake; under Elizabeth I ministers of religion who attempted to conduct services other than those authorized by the official Prayer Book could be sentenced to life imprisonment for a third offence; under the *Act for Restraining the Queen's Subjects in their due Obedience*, passed in 1593, anyone who refused to attend his or her parish church for a month was liable to imprisonment, and anyone who refused to conform within three months was given the choice of exile or death. Dissenters consequently did not court publicity.

Separatists of the sixteenth and early seventeenth centuries had two distinct lines of descent: radicals who traced their spiritual ancestry back to the Lollards of the fifteenth century, who were influenced by the continental Anabaptists from the 1530s onwards, and who looked forward to the General Baptists and Quakers of the seventeenth century, and Calvinistic Puritans who were disillusioned with the Church of England as it was restored by Elizabeth I and Parliament in 1559. Documentary evidence of the radical tradition of Dissent is so elusive before the

1640s that some historians have denied that any continuity can be traced: we have evidence of Anabaptists who were burned alive in the reign of Henry VIII, of sectarian opponents of predestination who met in Bocking in Essex and in Maidstone and Ashford in Kent in the early 1550s and whose imprisonment and subsequent martyrdom were recorded by Foxe's *Acts and Monuments of the English Martyrs*, and of the heretic Edward Wightman who was burned at Lichfield in 1612. But the strongest evidence linking the Lollards of the fifteenth century and the Anabaptists of the sixteenth century with the later General Baptists is geographic: one of the first General Baptist churches in England, in existence by 1626, was founded in the old Lollard centre of Coventry; in the 1640s and 1650s General Baptist ideas made rapid headway in the Weald of Kent and the Chilterns of Buckinghamshire; and General Baptists also became fairly strong in the clothing towns of northern Essex around Bocking. Local historians have noted that the very names of the persecuted Lollards of the first two decades of the sixteenth century reappear in General Baptist records a century and a half later.[2] Any historian who can find other evidence to support the thesis of continuity between the Lollards and the General Baptists will be making a considerable contribution to the history of Dissent.

We have more evidence of the second, Calvinist tradition of sixteenth-century and early seventeenth-century Dissent, but again we know of the existence of many of its adherents only from the records of their persecutors. Much of the available evidence is in the Harleian manuscripts and the Boswell papers in the British Library and in the State Papers in the Public Record Office and was published by Champlin Burrage in 1912 in his two-volume *Early English Dissenters*. Burrage's documents show how attempts by Elizabeth I to enforce the ceremonies prescribed by the Prayer Book of 1559 drove extreme Puritans to meet in private conventicles, beginning with seventeen who were arrested for meeting in the Plumbers' Hall in the City of London in 1567. Four years later we have evidence, from a petition to the queen, of the oldest known organized Separatist church in England, but the fragmentary nature of the evidence for Elizabethan Separatism is revealed by the fact that the first we know about the church's pastor, Richard Fitz, is that by 1571 he had already died of 'long imprisonment'.[3]

The historian is on firmer ground with the formation of a Separatist church in Norwich in 1581 by the two quarrelsome school teachers Robert Browne and Robert Harrison. After two periods of imprisonment persuaded Browne and his followers to take refuge in Middelburg in the Netherlands Browne and Harrison found in the Low Countries the freedom to publish their views which was denied them in England. Their writings constitute the first substantial corpus by English Dissenters. *The Writings of Robert Harrison and Robert Browne*, edited by Albert Peel and Leland Carlson, were reprinted in 1953, and other works by early Separatist leaders, some of which appeared first from Dutch printing presses, have also been reprinted. These include the writings of Henry Barrow and John Greenwood, both executed at Tyburn in 1593 for devising 'seditious books', and the works of John Smyth, once Fellow of Christ's College, Cambridge,[4] who was elected pastor by a group of Separatists which met at Gainsborough in Lincoln-

shire and fled to Amsterdam in 1608. Once in Amsterdam Smyth rejected both infant baptism and, probably under the influence of the Mennonite Anabaptists, the Calvinist doctrines of predestined election and reprobation. Smyth himself joined the Mennonites but some of his followers, led by Thomas Helwys, returned to England to found, at Spitalfields in 1612, the first General Baptist church on English soil. A second group of Separatists from the lower Trent valley, led by another former Cambridge don John Robinson, also emigrated to the Netherlands in 1608. Robinson settled in Leyden in 1609 and died there sixteen years later, but some of his followers left the Netherlands in 1620 to sail by way of Southampton and Plymouth to the New World and to come down in history as the Pilgrim Fathers.

Because so many English Separatists sought refuge in the Netherlands and New England, and because those Separatists who risked their lives by remaining or returning to England were obliged to keep their activities secret, the local historian who seeks to trace the early history of Dissent in his locality is likely to meet with frustration. But the extent to which dissatisfaction with a persecuting State Church was bubbling under the surface of English religious life was revealed when the authority of State and Church collapsed in the early 1640s. With the summoning of the Long Parliament in 1640, the collapse of episcopal authority in 1641, and the outbreak of the Civil War in 1642, Separatists were now free to meet in conventicles, heretics to propound unorthodox religious views, and sceptics to question the teachings of the Church. After a dearth of historical material the historian of Dissent is presented with a mass of evidence thrown up by the new-found freedom of religion.

Much of this material, numbering 22,000 items in all, was collected by the London bookseller George Thomason and is now housed in the British Library in London.[5] And some of it consists of the hysterical reactions of Royalists like John Taylor and Presbyterians like Thomas Edwards who regarded with horror the *Swarme of Sectaries, and Schismatiques* who were once no more than 'a handful and then crept in corners', but were now like 'the Egyptian locust covering the land'.[6] The horror stories retailed by Taylor and Edwards cannot necessarily he taken at face value, but Edwards, in compiling his *Gangraena, or a Catalogue of Discovery of many of the Errors, Heresies, Blasphemies and pernicious practices of the Sectaries* of this time, was in correspondence with fellow ministers in many parts of the country. As a result Edwards's *Gangraena*, if used critically, can be a mine of information for the local historian. He provides us with the first evidence of the spread of religious Dissent throughout much of England.

We are not, though, reliant for evidence for this upsurge of religious enthusiasm solely on the testimony of opponents. The collapse of press censorship meant that for the first time Dissenters were free to publish their views in England and many of the resulting publications have also found their way into the Thomason collection. Dissenters were also free, for the first time, to form gathered churches in England without fear of persecution. Some of these churches, those of the General Baptists, were in the radical tradition and rejected any ties between Church and State. Others, those of the Congregationalists, were in the Calvinist Puritan tradition and often tried to combine the principle of the gathered church with the use of parish churches and the continued maintenance of ministers of religion by tithes. The Particular Baptists, who differed from the Congregationalists by their insistence on believers' baptism and from the General

Baptists by their adherence to the Calvinist doctrine of predestination, straddled the radical and Puritan traditions with some of their ministers acting as parish ministers. But all three denominations have records going back to at least the 1650s, records which refute the arguments of those historians who maintain that denominational distinctions cannot be found in the Interregnum. Thirty General Baptist churches in the Midlands came together in 1651 to draw up a confession of faith and three years later the records of the General Baptist Assembly begin when representatives from 'several parts of this nation' met in London.[7] The oldest extant records of an individual General Baptist church are those of the Fenstanton church in Huntingdonshire which begin in 1651 and were published by the Hanserd Knollys Society in 1854.[8] The records of the Broadmead Particular Baptist church in Bristol begin with a historical introduction which starts in 1640, though the accuracy of this introduction has been questioned, and these records have also been published.[9] And while the Particular Baptists did not meet in national assembly until 1689, they had regional associations, the earliest of which contained representatives from churches in south Wales who met first in 1650.[10] The Congregationalists similarly did not have a national gathering until representatives of over a hundred churches met at the Savoy palace in London in 1658, but they, too, have records of individual churches dating back to the 1640s. The records of the joint Yarmouth-Norwich church begin in 1643 and, along with other early records of East Anglian Congregational churches, were transcribed in the eighteenth century by Thomas Harmer, minister of the Congregational church at Wattisfield in Suffolk. These records are now preserved in Dr. Williams's Library in London and provide a valuable insight into the life and work of

From Lucifers Lacky in the Thomason Collection in the British Library.
The illustration shows a tub preacher addressing a Separatist
congregation and probably represents the cobbler Samuel How.
How argued that it was the Holy Spirit, not human learning, that
qualified a man to understand and preach the gospel.

When Women Preach, and Coblers Pray,
The fiends in Hell, make holiday.

Congregational churches in the 1640s and 1650s.

In the turmoil of the Civil War and Interregnum new radical sects appeared — Ranters, Diggers, Muggletonians — most of which disappeared within a few years,[11] but one new sect prospered and survived: the Quakers. One reason for Quaker success was the personality of the movement's founder, George Fox, who travelled throughout much of England repudiating what he saw as the formalism of other Christian groups and offering to every man and woman the prospect of enlightenment 'by the divine light of Christ'. Fox's Journal is valuable to the local historian not only for the light it sheds on the early history of the Quaker movement but also for the insight it provides, albeit extremely critical, of religious life in England during the Interregnum. Because the appeal of the Quakers threatened all other religious groups — radical sects such as the General Baptists in particular provided the Quakers with many recruits — their appearance produced an enormous literature both in support of and in opposition to their claims. Much of this pamphlet literature is in the Thomason collection in the British Library and some has been republished by H. Barbour and A. O. Roberts under the title *Early Quaker Writings*. The success of the local historian in tracing the origins of Nonconformity in his neighbourhood will thus depend very much on his locality: if, for example, he is concerned with the origins of the Congregationalists of East Anglia, the Particular Baptists of south Wales or Bristol, the General Baptists of Huntingdonshire or Kent, the Quakers of the Midlands or Cumbria, or the Dissenters of any of the older denominations in London, he is likely to find material for his researches stretching back to the Interregnum or even earlier.

The return of Charles II in 1660 and the re-establishment of the episcopal Church of England presented Dissenters both with new challenges and with new opportunities: challenges because with the legislation of the Clarendon Code there was a return to the religious persecution of the days of Elizabeth and the first two Stuarts, opportunities because the insistence that every minister of the Church of England should declare his 'unfeigned assent and consent' to the Book of Common Prayer led to the ejection from their livings of over two thousand Puritan clergy who had hitherto sought to reform the Church of England from within. Of these ejected clergymen 194 were Congregationalists and another 19 were Baptists, but the vast majority were reforming clergymen who had hitherto eschewed denominational labels but who now took to themselves the name of Presbyterian. That the humble Baptists and despised Quakers were now joined, as Dissenters, by the over two thousand educated clergymen and their followers was a powerful aid in their resistance to the new wave of persecution. The third Edmund Calamy, grandson of one of the ejected ministers of 1662, collected the biographies of many of the dispossessed clergymen and his collection, supplemented by A.G. Matthews, R.T. Jones, and B. G. Owens, is an essential starting point for any historian working on post-1660 Dissent.[12]

The records of the renewed persecution provide the historian with a fund of information on the life of Dissent under Charles II. Most County Record Offices hold Quarter Sessions rolls in which were entered presentments of men and women who refused to attend services at their parish church. The State Papers in the Public Record Office contain much evidence of the persecution of Nonconformists, and a very full abstract of the documents is provided in the published *Calendars of State Papers Domestic*. When Charles II temporarily suspended the penal laws against Dissenters in 1672 congregations which wanted to take advantage of the Indulgence were required to take out licences, both for their meeting places and for their preachers. Details of these licences were published by G. Lyon Turner in his *Original Records of Early Nonconformity* (3 vols., 1911-12) and are a valuable source of information.

The historian who seeks to study Nonconformity in his own neighbourhood should always start with statistics: with ascertaining the size of the local Dissenting community, with trying to find out how its support fluctuated over the years, with estimating how significant a proportion of the total population of the locality it constituted. The earliest source which enables such calculations to be made is the inquiry launched by Bishop Compton of London in 1676. Bishop Compton, acting at the behest of the Lord Treasurer, the Earl of Danby, asked the bishops of the province of Canterbury to obtain from their clergy an estimate of the number of persons residing within their parishes and of the number of Dissenters 'who either obstinately refuse or wholly absent themselves from the communion of the Church of England'. A similar survey was conducted in the province of York, though the returns have survived for only two of the four northern dioceses, York and

Carlisle, and the results of all these surveys have now been published.[13] Interpreting the so-called Compton census is difficult: clergy were confused as to whether children should or should not be counted, and in the diocese of Worcester the clergy often counted only men. The clergy were not asked to give the denomination of the Dissenters within their parishes, and their terms of reference excluded many occasional conformists who would subsequently be found in Presbyterian congregations. But the Compton census provides the first statistical evidence to enable the historian to assess the strength of Dissent in his locality.

The records of the Dissenting churches themselves for the most part fall silent for the period of the Caroline persecution, but those of the Broadmead Baptist church in Bristol provide a valuable picture of the way in which one Dissenting congregation coped with the years of persecution. Unlike many Dissenters the Quakers refused 'to dodge and shift' to avoid persecution, and when Quaker meeting-houses were closed or pulled down Friends continued to meet in the street or amongst the rubble of their demolished buildings. As a result Quakers suffered more than members of other denominations and records of their persecution were gathered by Joseph Besse in his *Collection of the Sufferings of the People called Quakers* in 1753. One reason for Quaker survival was the superb organization built up by George Fox in the 1660s with a hierarchy of meetings rising from particular meetings for worship to Monthly Meetings for discipline, county Quarterly Meetings, and the national Yearly Meeting. At the apex stood the Meeting for Sufferings, established in 1675 to secure relief from persecution, which became the executive committee of English Quakerism. All these meetings kept their own records, and some date from the

period of persecution. The minute books of the Bedfordshire Quarterly Meeting, housed in the Hertfordshire County Record Office, begin in 1668, and those of the Durham Quarterly Meeting, preserved in the Friends Meeting House in Darlington, date from 1671.[14] Others, such as the *Minute Book of the Men's Meeting of the Society of Friends in Bristol, 1667-86* (Bristol Record Society, 1971), *The First Minute Book of the Gainsborough Monthly Meeting of the Society of Friends, 1669-1719* (Lincolnshire Record Society, 1939), and *The Somerset Quarterly Meeting of the Society of Friends, 1668-1600* (Somerset Record Society, 1978) have been published.

After one final, savage burst of persecution between 1681 and 1685, the death of Charles II and his Roman Catholic brother James's desire to unite Catholics and Dissenters against the Church of England brought first temporary relief to Nonconformists and, after the overthrow of James II, permanent toleration. The Toleration Act of 1689 allowed freedom of worship to Dissenters provided that they took the oaths of allegiance and supremacy and obtained a licence for their meetings. From 1689 until 1852 every Nonconformist meeting had to be registered, either by the local bishop, archdeacon, or magistrates, and this system of licensing provides another essential source for historians wishing to trace the story of their local Nonconformist communities. Certificates issued under the Toleration Act can be found in both county and diocesan record offices though, like all such records, they must be treated critically since the denominational labels the licensing authorities fixed to congregations were often wrong.[15] And with the toleration of Dissent came another important piece of historical evidence: the visible construction of Nonconformist meeting-houses. Those few meeting-houses that have survived

Taunton Unitarian chapel, Somerset, built in 1721. Unlike most future Unitarian churches, Taunton originated as a General Baptist, not a Presbyterian, meeting. Interior sketch by H. Godwin Arnold.

from the late seventeenth and early eighteenth centuries have received belated recognition from architectural historians as superb examples of vernacular architecture and they have been the subject of several attractively produced volumes: K. Lindley, *Chapels and Meeting Houses* (1969); A. Jones, *Welsh Chapels* (Cardiff, 1984); G. and J. Hague, *The Unitarian Heritage, an Architectural Survey* (Sheffield, 1986); and the two magnificent volumes produced by Christopher Stell for the Royal Commission on Historic Monuments, *Nonconformist Chapels and Meeting-Houses in Central England* (1986), and *in South-West England* (1991).

The importance, for Dissenters, of the addition of the often wealthy Presbyterians to the ranks of the humbler Congregationalists, Baptists, and Quakers is illustrated by the foundation of the most important library for the study of the history of Dissent, Dr Williams's Library in Gordon Square, London. Daniel Williams, minister to the Hand Alley Presbyterian meeting in London, acquired great wealth through two fortunate marriages and since neither marriage produced children he left, on his death in 1716, £50,000 in trust for educational and religious purposes and for the library that bears his name. That library contains much crucial material for the local historian of Dissent. The Toleration Act of 1689 was followed by attempts at union between Presbyterians and Congregationalists and by the setting up, in 1690, of a Common Fund by Presbyterian and Congregational ministers in London to assist poorer Dissenting congregations and ministers in the country. The attempted 'Happy Union' in London soon foundered on the rocks of a theological controversy in which Daniel Williams himself played a leading part, but not before managers of the Common Fund had conducted a survey of Presbyterian and Congregational churches

throughout the country in an attempt to discover those that were in need of financial assistance. The manuscript of this survey is housed in Dr Williams's Library and was published by Alexander Gordon in 1917 under the title *Freedom after Election*. Outside London attempts to secure Presbyterian-Congregational co-operation were more enduring in Devon and Lancashire and the resulting minutes of the Exeter and Lancashire Assemblies are available to the local historian. The minutes of the Exeter Assembly have been published and those of the Lancashire Assembly can be consulted in Dr. Williams's Library.[16]

A source of even greater importance is the survey conducted by Daniel Williams's successor at the Hand Alley Presbyterian meeting, John Evans, between 1715 and 1718. The survey seems to have been prompted by a threatened return of persecution with the Schism Act of 1714 which forbade anyone who attended Dissenting meetings to teach on pain of three months in prison. John Evans, who was secretary of the Committee of the Three Denominations of Presbyterians, Congregationalists, and Baptists, set up in 1702 to protect Dissenting interests, wrote to correspondents throughout England and Wales asking for the location of every Dissenting congregation, the name of its minister, and the number and 'quality' of his 'hearers'. The resulting information, which is also housed in Dr. Williams's Library, constitutes the most comprehensive survey of Dissent we have before the religious census of 1851. And although the accuracy of the statistics in the Evans list has sometimes been questioned, comparison with other contemporary sources such as episcopal visitation returns suggests that the list is a substantially reliable base from which to calculate the strength of Dissent in the early eighteenth century.[17] Those visitation returns, which often contain estimates by parish clergy of the number of Dissenters in their parishes, are another useful source of information. Some of these visitation returns have been published[18] and others can be found in county and diocesan record offices.

In addition to asking his correspondents to list the number of hearers in Dissenting congregations in their counties, Dr Evans also asked them to tell him the number of Nonconformists in each congregation who possessed the right to vote, and in recent years historians have been paying increasing attention to the political importance of Dissent in the late seventeenth and eighteenth centuries. Studies by Gary de Krey and James Bradley suggest that Dissenters, although very largely excluded from national politics, played an important role in the local politics of numerous towns.[19] De Krey, working on London in the period between the Glorious Revolution and the death of Queen Anne, and Bradley, working on the country at large in the 1770s and 1780s, have both found that 'the Dissenters provided the Whigs with their most reliable political constituency'.[20] The local historian of Nonconformity is thus faced with the challenge not only of tracing the growth of Dissent in his area and of assessing its numerical strength, he is also confronted with the task of assessing its political influence.

Unitarians and Evangelicals, 1730-1851

Despite the toleration they had enjoyed since 1689, and despite the wealth of at least some Dissenting congregations revealed by the Common Fund Survey and the Evans list, it was clear that by the 1730s the Dissenting interest was declining.[21] It was a decline that much exercised the minds of contemporary Dissenters, but it was not one to which many historians have addressed themselves and it is a topic on which a study of local sources could yield fresh information. Many eighteenth-century Congregationalists thought they knew the reason for the decline of Dissent: the tendency for Presbyterian and General Baptist ministers and congregations to embrace first Arian and later Socinian views. As a consequence of departing from orthodox Trinitarian theology, claimed their critics, Presbyterians and General Baptists lost the Evangelical zeal that motivated the Particular Baptists and Congregationalists and as a result they failed to win new adherents. The Evans list of 1715-18 had revealed the existence of nearly 180,000 Presbyterians in 637 meetings, making them the largest Dissenting denomination of the day and constituting 3.3 per cent of the total population of England. But by 1851 there were only 202 Unitarian congregations in England, the vast majority of them descended from Presbyterian meetings of the previous century. And while at the same time there were 142 orthodox Presbyterian congregations in England, most of them composed largely of immigrant Scots, Presbyterians and Unitarians together in 1851 numbered only 84,190, a mere 0.5 per cent of England's total population. There is thus a considerable amount of statistical evidence to suggest a decline from eighteenth-century Presbyterianism to nineteenth-century Unitarianism for the local historian to explain. A similar decline afflicted the Quakers, who shared many of the social, if not theological, characteristics of the Unitarians. The number of their adherents in England declined from over 39,000 in 1715-18 to under 17,000 in 1851, a decrease from 0.7 to 0.1 per cent of the total population.[22] Again the decline of the Society of Friends represents a challenge to the local historian to chart and explain.

By contrast with the decline of the Presbyterian/Unitarians and Quakers, the Evangelical Dissenters, the Congregationalists and Baptists, experienced spectacular growth in the late eighteenth and first half of the nineteenth centuries. In 1772-3 the Baptist pastor Josiah Thompson made another attempt to survey the number of Dissenting congregations in England and Wales and the results of his findings are also in Dr Williams's Library, along with the manuscript history of some hundred congregations in five volumes.[23] It is possible to compare Thompson's list with that of John Evans and with the religious census of 1851 to gauge the extent of the growth of Evangelical Nonconformity at both local and national level. Whereas comparison between the Thompson list and the Evans list suggests that there may have been a hundred fewer Dissenting congregations in England and Wales in 1772-3 than in 1715-18, comparison between the Thompson list and the 1851 religious census suggests that in the eighty years from 1772 the number of Nonconformist congregations increased ten-fold. Whereas there were perhaps 300 Congregational churches in 1772-3, by 1851 there were 3,244 Congregational places of worship. Whereas Josiah Thompson listed 402 Baptist congregations, the 1851 census listed 2,789. While the Nonconformists constituted just over 6 per cent of the population of England in 1715-18, and rather less than 6 per cent of the population of Wales, by 1851 Nonconformists constituted 17 per cent of the population of England and 45 per cent of the population of Wales.[24] But the enormous increase in the strength of Nonconformity was only partly due to the exertions of the Baptists and the Congregationalists: by 1851 just over half the Nonconformists of England and nearly half the Nonconformists of Wales belonged to the new denominations produced by the Evangelical revival: the Methodists. These included not only the original Methodist connexions which dated from the 1730s, the Calvinistic Methodists (predominantly in Wales) and the Wesleyan Methodists, but also the numerous denominations formed by secession from the Arminian Methodists in the sixty years following Wesley's death: the Methodist New Connexion, the Primitive Methodists, the Bible Christians, the Wesleyan Methodist Association, and the Wesleyan Reformers. The religious census showed that over a third of all worshippers at Arminian Methodist chapels in England and Wales attended the services of one of these break-away Methodist denominations.

The published returns to the 1851 religious census give the denominational totals of both chapels and attenders for each of 624 registration districts, but the original returns in the Public Record Office provide valuable information on virtually every Nonconformist chapel (and Anglican parish church) in England and Wales. The original returns for Bedford-shire, Buckinghamshire, Hampshire, Lincolnshire, Nottinghamshire, Oxfordshire, Sussex, and Wales have all been published, thus facilitating the study of Dissent at local level. As is so often the case, interpreting this statistical material is not easy because clergymen and ministers were asked to provide estimates of the size of their congregations at morning, afternoon, and evening services, and no attempt was made to find out how many people attended church or chapel more than once on census Sunday. However the difficulty can be resolved by taking the figure for the best-attended service at each place of worship and adding a third of the total number of worshippers at the less well-attended services. This formula is consistent with the views often expressed by ministers of religion who filled in the census returns and is also consistent with what information we have about the membership of individual churches.[25] Armed with estimates of the number of people actually worshipping in Nonconformist chapels on census Sunday, the local historian can relate this information to the size of towns and villages, their land holding patterns, and the strength of the Church of England.[26] The geographic distribution of Dissent can then be plotted on maps, and such maps enable the local historian to address one of the vexed questions of Nonconformist historiography: whether Nonconformity expanded by taking advantage of the failure of the Church of England to cope with the demographic changes of the late eighteenth and early nineteenth centuries, or whether it flourished in places where the religious seed had in fact been sown by the established church. In Nottinghamshire, whereas the Congregationalists flourished in urban centres such as Newark, Mansfield, and Nottingham itself, and the General Baptists of the New Connexion had their largest following in towns and

John Wesley addressing Methodist preachers in City Road Chapel, London
Wesley's Chapel

industrial villages, all areas where the Church of England was comparatively weak, the Methodists made their greatest impact in rural areas where the Church of England was also strong.[27] The situation in Nottinghamshire was thus almost the exact reverse of the theory postulated by Robert Currie, that whereas Old Dissent 'grew strong where the Church of England was strong ... Methodism grew strong where the Church of England was weak'.[28] And it is not only the relationship between Nonconformity and the Church of England that the local historian needs to investigate. Recent studies by James Obelkevich on south Lindsey in Lincolnshire, by John Rule on Cornwall, and by David Clarke on the North Riding fishing village of Staithes all suggest that the growth of Methodism may have been

facilitated not so much by the teaching of the Church of England as by the survival of pre-Christian pagan superstition.[29] Here is another important historical issue to which the local historian may be able to make a distinctive contribution.

Another issue which the local historian is well placed to tackle concerns the social structure of Nonconformity. Many historians have argued that nineteenth-century Nonconformity was predominantly middle-class, while Alan Gilbert maintained that Nonconformity had a particular appeal to the independent artisan, and a few historians have concluded from detailed local studies that the social structure of Nonconformist congregations was very like that of the communities from which they were drawn.[30] My own researches suggest that while Dissent in the late seventeenth and eighteenth centuries drew its support chiefly from the economically independent, from merchants, tradesmen, artisans, and rural freeholders, the huge expansion of Evangelical Nonconformity between 1780 and 1840 was made possible by attracting a growing number of unskilled and semi-skilled workers and their wives. While a minority of Dissenting congregations — Quaker, Unitarian, and sometimes Congregational — were very prosperous, the overwhelming majority of Nonconformist churches were made up of poor people. Only in the 1840s is there substantial evidence to suggest that urban, though not rural, Evangelical Nonconformity was becoming more bourgeois.[31]

Some historians have used chapel trust deeds in attempts to ascertain the social status of Dissenting congregations, but such deeds are of limited use since chapel trustees were chosen from among the more prosperous members of any congregation, though chapel trust deeds which include the names of a number of unskilled and semi-skilled workers are clear evidence that the membership as a whole was very poor.[32] A much more reliable source for determining the social structure of Nonconformist congregations are the birth and baptismal registers which were collected by the registrar general following the establishment of the Civil Registry of Births, Marriages, and Deaths in 1836. Some 9,000 Nonconformist registers are housed in the Public Record Office, of these over 4,500 are birth and baptismal registers, and nearly half of them contain evidence of the occupations of the fathers of the children whose births are registered therein.[33] It has sometimes been argued that the parents who had their children's births recorded in Nonconformist baptismal registers were not necessarily connected to the chapel concerned, but the internal evidence of some registers, which state whether the parents were or were not members of the church or congregation, and comparison with church membership lists suggest that the baptismal registers accurately

reflect the occupational profile of the congregations to which they belonged.[34] Unfortunately the Public Record Office's holding of Nonconformist baptismal registers comes to an almost complete halt in 1837, but registers for subsequent decades are preserved in virtually every County Record Office and by many individual churches.

The Nonconformist birth and baptismal registers are a mine of information for the local historian. They enable the researcher not only to analyze the occupational structure of many congregations, they provide him with vital information with which to compare with other contemporary sources such as trade directories, probate records, and poll books. One of the major problems posed by the use of the descriptions of fathers' occupations in baptismal registers to ascertain the social structure of any Nonconformist congregation is the knowledge that terms such as 'cotton spinner', 'brewer', or 'tailor' can be used both of prosperous employers and of poorly paid employees. The historian who seeks to use this material on a national scale can only make intelligent guesses on the basis of probability as to which social classes such men belonged, but the local historian can more accurately analyze the social structure of single congregations by using trade directories and probate records in an attempt to discover the social standing of men whose classification is not immediately apparent from the description of their occupation.

Similarly the names of fathers in baptismal registers can be matched with poll books to discover whether they were of sufficient social standing to qualify for the vote and to discover their political loyalties. Until 1872 voting in England and Wales was open and in the smaller boroughs in particular local printers often found it worth their while to publish lists of voters and the way they had cast their votes.[35] Such lists are often to be found in the local history sections of local libraries and, in conjunction with baptismal registers and membership lists, can be used to establish the way Nonconformists voted. The researcher is likely to find that most Old Dissenters — Baptists, Congregationalists, Quakers, and Unitarians — supported Whig or Liberal candidates, but the electoral preference of Methodist voters is much more difficult to predict. While members of the secessionist Methodist denominations, the New Connexion Methodists, the Wesleyan Methodist Association, and the Wesleyan Reformers, were likely to favour Liberal rather than Conservative candidates, the leaders of the Wesleyan and Calvinistic Methodist often prided themselves on their support for the established church and the Tory party. There is some evidence that by the later 1830s members of the Wesleyan and Calvinistic Methodist rank-and-file were rebelling against the

pro-Tory sympathies of their leaders and supporting the Liberals.[36] Only detailed research by local historians can establish the extent to which this was a widespread trend.

While recent research has emphasized the political importance of Nonconformity even in the eighteenth century, the rapid expansion of Dissent in the first half of the nineteenth century, coupled with the Reform Act of 1832 and the Municipal Corporations Act of 1835, meant that for the rest of the century Nonconformity was to be an increasingly significant political force. The most important source for understanding that significance is the periodical press. The late eighteenth and first half of the nineteenth centuries saw a vast increase in the numbers of newspapers and magazines published, and a significant proportion of those publications were owned and edited by Nonconformists. In town after town Dissenters founded journals to campaign against the disabilities suffered by Nonconformists and on behalf of other liberal causes. Papers such as the *Cambridge Intelligencer*, the *Leeds Mercury*, the *Leicester Chronicle*, the

Water Street Calvinistic Methodist chapel, Carmarthen, 1813. From a wood engraving by Hugh Hughes.

23

Manchester Guardian, the *Nottingham Review*, the *Sheffield Independent*, and the *Tyne Mercury* were all edited by Nonconformists, and their files provide the local historian with a valuable insight into the political opinions and activities of Dissenters. In addition every Nonconformist denomination had at least one regularly published periodical — the *Wesleyan Methodist Magazine*, the *Primitive Methodist Magazine*, the *Congregational Magazine*, the *Baptist Magazine*, *Y Drysorfa* (Calvinistic Methodist), *Seren Gomer* (Welsh Baptist), and *Y Dysgedydd* (Welsh Independent), and so on — and by 1850 at least thirty-nine such periodicals were in existence.[37] Such magazines provide a fund of information for the local historian, with evidence of religious revivals, the founding of chapels, and the appointment and departure of ministers. Particularly important are the accounts of religious experience and the obituaries which provide insights into the motives that prompted individual men and women to join Nonconformist churches. And uniting the features, and much of the information, of the provincial newspapers and the denominational magazines are the religious newspapers such as the *Patriot* (moderate Dissenting), the *Nonconformist* (radical Dissenting), the *Watchman* (Tory Wesleyan), and the *Wesleyan Chronicle* (Liberal Wesleyan). Sifting through file after file of newspapers is time-consuming and exhausting, and for that reason historians do not do it as often as they should. But the periodical press constitutes the single most important source for the study of nineteenth-century Nonconformity.

Dissent was a public cause, religiously and politically, and for that reason its most important opinions and activities were reported in the press. But it also had a private side, recorded in church minute books, circuit records, and private correspondence. Whereas such records are rare

for the Interregnum and scarce for the period following the Toleration Act, the local historian is likely to find an enormous quantity of material for the late eighteenth and nineteenth centuries. Every County Record Office has its collection of church minute books and Methodist circuit records; many churches still preserve their own records; and national repositories such as the National Library of Wales, the Angus Library of Regent's Park College in Oxford and the Baptist headquarters at Didcot, the Congregational Library housed in Dr Williams's Library, the Friends House Library in Euston Road, and the Methodist archives in the John Rylands Library in Manchester also house manuscript records. The John Rylands Library has an extensive collection of the correspondence of Methodist preachers which, given the peripatetic nature of the Methodist ministry, is of particular importance for the local historian.[38] John Wesley's *Journal* (8 vols., ed. N. Curnock, 1909-16) and *Letters* (8 vols., ed. J. Telford, 1931) have been published, and both are being republished in a new series by Oxford University Press (ed. Frank Baker). Much of the correspondence of Jabez Bunting has also been published under the titles *The Early Correspondence of Jabez Bunting, 1820-29*, (Camden Fourth Series, vol. 11, 1972) and *Early Victorian Methodism, 1830-58* (Oxford, 1976). A guide to the correspondence of two hundred other prominent Nonconformist (and also Anglican) leaders is provided by *Papers of British Churchmen, 1780-1940*, published by the Royal Commission on Historical Manuscripts in 1987.

Church and circuit minute books and the correspondence of denominational leaders enable the local historian to build up a picture of life at chapel level: of relations between ministers and their congregations, of the financing of ministerial salaries and chapel building, of the disciplining of church members. However the historian must be ever mindful of the fact that such sources by their very nature record the unusual rather than the customary, disputes rather than harmony, financial crises rather than the regularity of worship. In order to recapture the flavour of nineteenth-century Nonconformity the local historian should also seek out the biographies and autobiographies of the very many denominational leaders and humble laymen, and sometimes women, who have left behind a record of their lives. And the local historian would also be advised to use as his model one of the many excellent existing local histories of Nonconformist communities. Unfortunately most of the best work is in the form of university theses and has never been published.[39] A guide to these dissertations is provided by *Historical Research for Higher Degrees in the United Kingdom*, published annually by the Institute of Historical Research. Of published work Alan Brockett's *Nonconformity in Exeter* (1962) is an excellent example of the way in which the local study of Dissenting history should be tackled.

From the 1780s until the 1840s the history of Nonconformity was one of rapid and almost uninterrupted growth. But in the 1840s all the Nonconformist denominations started to complain of slowing rates of growth and even of declining numbers, and over the next hundred years Nonconformity experienced a decline in membership and ultimately of influence.

The rate of decline and its causes are difficult to establish. By a remarkable coincidence the total membership of all the Nonconformist churches in England and Wales reached its peak in 1906, the year in which they also gained their greatest political triumph as part of the Liberal landslide of that year. Membership figures for the Baptists and Wesleyan Methodists both reached their zenith in 1906, the Free Methodists reached their maximum membership in 1907, and the Congregationalists and Primitive Methodists both peaked in 1908.[40] Thereafter the membership figures for all the denominations have declined up to the present day. But these are absolute figures, not membership expressed as a percentage of the total population, and calculating when Nonconformists per head of population began to decline is rendered difficult by the fact that neither the Particular Baptists nor the Congregationalists kept accurate membership figures at national level before the 1890s. However all the Methodist denominations kept membership figures throughout their history and by combining these and presenting them as a percentage of the total population over the age of 15, we can have some idea of when Nonconformity

began to decline in real terms. Combined Arminian Methodist membership per head of adult population in England and Wales rose steadily from 1.61 per cent in 1801 to 3.37 per cent in 1831. The 1830s saw a spectacular rise in Methodist membership which reached a peak of 4.47 per cent in 1841, but thereafter membership per head of population declined, a decline hastened by the bitter divisions which racked Wesleyan Methodism over the *Fly Sheets* controversy in 1849 and the secession of the Wesleyan Reformers. Methodist membership figures recovered with the religious revival of the late 1850s and by 1863 there were 4.25 Methodists per 100 people over the age of 15. The Methodists managed to retain the membership of 4 per cent of the adult population for most of the 1870s and 1880s, but thereafter decline once again set in, falling to 3.80 per cent by 1891, to 3.27 per cent by 1911, and to 2.71 per cent by 1931.[41] In Wales the pattern may have been different, with Nonconformists per head of population reaching a peak in 1881, holding steady for twenty years, and then declining from the first decade of the twentieth century onwards.[42] But whatever the national picture, the local historian will want to establish the pattern of growth and decline in his or her own neighbourhood, using the membership figures preserved in church minute books and in the various denominational yearbooks.

There was no national census of religious worship in England between 1851 and 1979, but for Wales the historian can turn to the statistics collected in 1905 by the Royal Commission on the Church of England and Other Religious Bodies. The evidence was published in a volume entitled *Nonconformist County Statistics* which provides details of the accommodation, adherents, and communicants in every chapel in Wales.[43] And in England at the end of 1881 a number of local newspapers conducted their own religious censuses and the results were collected by the *Nonconformist and Independent* in February 1882 and summarised in Andrew Mearns's *Statistics of Attendance at Public Worship, 1881-2.* The historian of London is especially fortunate in having at his disposal two censuses of attendance for the late nineteenth and early twentieth centuries: the *British Weekly's* census of 1886-7, and the census conducted by the *Daily News* in 1902-3 and published by Richard Mudie-Smith under the title *The Religious Life of London* (1904). Finally the most sophisticated attempts yet made to determine the extent and nature of religious observance in England and Wales were made by the MARC Europe organization in 1979 and 1989. The surveys attempted to find out not only the level of church-going in each county but also church membership, the age and gender of congregations, and whether churches were growing or declining.[44] While there is thus much statistical evidence at the disposal of the local historian, there are also huge gaps in our knowledge of church- and chapel-going in the past which the local historian can play his or her part in filling.

Having collected his statistics, the local historian is faced with the daunting task of interpreting them. If the decline of Nonconformity relative to the total population did begin in the 1840s was this because, as has sometimes been claimed, the churches were alienating the working-class by their hostility to Chartism? Or was it, as the churches themselves were likely to argue, because the economic hardships of the 1840s were forcing poor men and women to relinquish their pews

and often their homeland? But if it was economic hardship that drove men and women away from organized religion, how does one reconcile this with the continuing decline for a century from the late 1880s onwards, a century of rising prosperity? Was it the very prosperity of the churches, with their more affluent congregations, their better-educated ministers, and their more dignified air that blunted their evangelistic zeal? Does the fact that the decline of church membership per head of population apparently dates from the late 1880s suggest that the most important factors were in the realm of ideas, the result of the weakening of faith induced by the publication of Darwin's *Origin of the Species* (1859) and the relaying of the results of German Biblical criticism to English readers through the medium of *Essays and Reviews* (1860)? Or does the coincidence of decline with attempts to form a separate working-class political party suggest that the close connection between Nonconformity and a Liberal party which prided itself on being above class conflict was the undoing of both? Did the growing tension between capital and labour tear the churches apart? Was it now impossible for Dissent to comprise, as it had for much of the nineteenth century, both captains of industry and leaders of the trade union movement? Why did the newest of the Evangelical Nonconformist denominations, the Salvation Army, not have the impact on the working class of the late nineteenth century that the Methodists had had half a century earlier? Did the very success of the Dissenting churches in helping working-class men and women to rise in the social scale lead to a widening gulf between the churches and the poor? Did the process of suburbanisation undermine attempts to evangelize the inner cities? Or was it the case, as was suggested by the *Daily News* census in London, that it was the middle classes rather than the working classes that were deserting the Nonconformist churches? Did churches of all denominations fail to retain the adherence of a majority of the population because they were unable to build sufficient buildings to accommodate the country's explosive rate of population growth?[45] Or did competitive church building produce too many half-empty churches and chapels whose very superabundance of accommodation was demoralizing to preachers and congregations alike?[46] Did the churches, in attuning their message to the evolutionary optimism of the late nineteenth and early twentieth centuries, leave their congregations unprepared to cope with the catastrophe of the First World War? Or was the decline in church membership already irreversible by 1914? These are crucial issues to which the local historian will have to address him or herself.[47]

The crisis which was afflicting Nonconformity in the late nineteenth century met with a vigorous response. Churches, hitherto primarily concerned with the saving of souls, addressed themselves increasingly to the care of bodies. Ministers such as the Baptist John Clifford and the Congregationalist Silvester Horne preached the social gospel, teaching that the mission of the churches was at least in part the achievement of a fairer society here on earth and not merely the salvation of the individual soul after death. The 1880s and the 1890s saw the widespread popularity of the 'institutional church', the surrounding of the worshipping community with a network of educational and social institutions intended to emphasize the relevance of Christianity to man's temporal existence and to attract and hold outsiders to the churches. Nonconformist churches offered Mutual Improvement Societies, evening classes, choral festivals, public lectures, savings banks, medical services, football, tennis and cricket clubs, and amateur dramatics. But the institutional church failed to prevent the decline of church membership from 1906 onwards. Was this because local authorities and professional entertainment promoters were providing better facilities than those offered by the churches? Or was it because the churches, by secularizing their message, were devaluing the essentials of the Christian faith? Was it a coincidence that the *Daily News* religious census in 1902-3 suggests that some of the most successful Nonconformist churches in London were conservative Baptist churches loyal to the 'fundamentalist' message preached by Charles Haddon Spurgeon'; or that the decline of the traditional Nonconformist denominations since the Second World War has been accompanied by the growth of the Pentecostal, charismatic, and house church movements, by the proliferation of independent Evangelical churches, and by the expansion of the Jehovah's Witnesses and the Mormons?

At the same time that the Nonconformist churches were seeking to make their message relevant to man's earthly concerns, they were also becoming increasingly involved in politics. The Municipal Corporations Act of 1835 had resulted in Dissenters becoming the dominant force in numerous borough councils and in the second half of the nineteenth century Nonconformists such as Joseph Chamberlain used their position in local politics as a springboard from which to enter national politics. Dissenters often took the lead in town improvements and it was but a short step from a 'civic gospel' emphasizing the churches' commitment to municipal reform to the Nonconformist conscience reflecting the ambition of the churches to control the life of the nation. In the last quarter of the nineteenth century Nonconformists opposed the medical inspection of prostitutes, agitated for restrictions on the opening hours of public houses, criticised the Prince of Wales for gambling and Lord

Clifford led the Nonconformists in their opposition to the 1902 Education Act which provided for support from the rates for Anglican and Roman Catholic schools. He also played a leading part in the general election of 1906 which gave the Liberals a huge majority.
Taken from the Pall Mall Gazette, May 9, 1906.

"OLIVER CROMWELL'S SUCCESSOR"

THE REV. CLIFFORD CROMWELL: "Take away that Bauble!"
[Mr. Lloyd-George says that "Dr. Clifford is the greatest Protestant since Oliver Cromwell." Mr. Balfour says: "This is what we have come to under Oliver Cromwell's successor."]

Rosebery for horse-racing, and tried to hound Sir Charles Dilke and Charles Stewart Parnell out of public life on account of their adultery. As the century progressed so the connections between the Nonconformist churches and the Liberal party became increasingly close. In the 1830s and 1840s the fundamental divide between Liberal and Conservative at grass-roots level was the issue of church rates — a tax imposed on all ratepayers, whether Anglican or Nonconformist, for the upkeep of the parish church. The church rates issue was resolved by their abolition in 1868, but only two years later the Education Act of 1870, by providing for the popular election of school boards, introduced another issue which would divide Liberal from Conservative, Dissenter from Anglican, at local level. The Liberal party's split over Irish Home Rule in 1886, by syphoning off some of its wealthier supporters, rendered the party even more dependent on Nonconformist support, and the links between the Liberal party and Dissent became closest in 1906, the year of the great Liberal landslide, when nearly half the 401 Liberal MPs elected were Nonconformists. The local historian will want to trace these links in his own area, using church minute books, the private papers of church leaders and politicians, but above all newspapers, both local and national. For the history of late nineteenth-century Nonconformity, as for the earlier part of the century, the most important single source is the periodical press, denominational papers such as the Baptist *Freeman* and the *Methodist*

Times, and the inter-denominational *British Weekly* and *Christian World*.

The general election of 1906 marked the apogee of both Liberal and Nonconformist political influence. The nature of that electoral victory, and the Nonconformists' role in it, has been the subject of controversy. Was it a victory for backward-looking causes such as free trade and undenominational education? Or did the Liberal-Nonconformist commitment to social reform herald the coming of the Welfare State? And the connection between the Liberal decline and Nonconformist decline is also one which the local historian will need to investigate: did the Free Churches, by emphasizing such irrelevant issues as disestablishment and such unpopular issues as temperance, alienate working-class men from the Liberal party? Or did the Liberal leaders, by tearing the party asunder during the First World War, leave the Dissenters without a natural political home? And what happened to Nonconformist political influence after 1918? Rather than decline with the Liberal party, did it now permeate both the Labour and Conservative parties? And was it for good or ill that Britain was led, between 1937 and 1940, by Neville Chamberlain, son of the former Unitarian mayor of Birmingham, and that even in the early 1980s the leaders of both the Conservative and Labour parties (Margaret Thatcher and Michael Foot) were the products of Methodist homes? If he or she can answer just some of these questions, the historian of the Nonconformist chapel will be making a real contribution to the history of the nation.

THE NEW INQUISITION

"It recalled the days when Puritanism reigned supreme in England, when, as Macaulay told them, it was a crime for a child to read by the bedside of a sick parent one of those beautiful Collects of the Prayer Book, which had soothed the griefs of forty generations of Christians." - Mr. F. G. Grant, J.P. at Burnley.

Brother Clifford: This, may it please the court, is a young pupil teacher who was caught in the act of reading to her innocent pupils that pernicious piece of literature-"The Book of Common Prayer." Brother Birrell: Dreadful! This calls for exemplary punishment.

THE NONCONFORMIST CONSCIENCE: THE PROSECUTION

Augustine Birrell, President of the Board of Education in the Liberal government of 1906, introduced a bill to curtail denominational religious instruction in schools receiving public money.

31

References

1. *E. Halévy*, **A History of the English People in 1815** (1924), 334-5, 339, 371.

2. *M.R. Watts*, **The Dissenters, i: From the Reformation to the French Revolution** (Oxford, 1978), 7-14, 283-4. Nesta Evans has recently found that of 59 Lollard surnames recorded in the Subsidy returns for twenty-one Buckinghamshire parishes in 1524, 48 (81 per cent) reappear as Baptists or Quakers in the Chiltern Hundreds in the 1660s, whereas only 29 per cent of all surnames found in 1524 recur 140 years later. *M. Spufford*, ed. **The World of Rural Dissenters, 1520-1725** (Cambridge, 1995), 296. *R.J. Acheson*, however, has been able to find little evidence of continuity between Lollard and Anabaptist influence in the Weald of Kent and the later concentration of General Baptist churches in the area. *Acheson*, **Radical Puritans in England, 1550-1660** (1990), 55.

3. *C. Burrage*, **Early English Dissenters** (Cambridge, 1912), ii. 15-18.

4. **The Writings of Henry Barrow, 1587-90**, ed. *L. Carlson* (1962); **The Writings of John Greenwood, 1587-90**, ed. *L. Carlson* (1962); **The Writings of Henry Barrow, 1590-1**, ed. *L. Carlson* (1966); **The Writings of John Greenwood and Henry Barrow 1591-93**, ed. *L. Carlson* (1970); **The Works of John Smyth** (2 vols), ed. *W.T. Whitley* (Cambridge, 1915).

5. See *G. K. Fortescue's* **Catalogue of the Pamphlets, Books, Newspapers, and Manuscripts ... collected by George Thomason** (2 vols., 1908). *J.F. McGregor* and *B. Reay*, **Radical Religion in the English Revolution** (Oxford, 1984), 13.

6. *J. Taylor*, **A Swarme of Sectaries, and Schismatiques** (1641). **Lucifer's Lacky** (1641), sig. A3.

7. **Minutes of the General Assembly of the General Baptist Churches in England, 1654-1811** (2 vols) ed. *W.T. Whitley* (1909-10), i. 1-5.

8. **Records of the Churches of Christ gathered at Fenstanton, Hexham, and Warboys, 1640-1720** ed. *E.B. Underhill* (1854).

9. **Records of a Church of Christ, meeting in Broadmead, Bristol, 1640-88**, ed. *N. Hayroft*, (1865); **The Records of a Church of Christ in Bristol**, ed. *R. Hayden*, (Bristol Record Society, 1974). The accuracy of the historical introduction to the Broadmead records has been questioned by *J. Wilson* in 'Another Look at John Canne', **Church History**, xxxiii (1964), 36-7.

10. **Association Records of the Particular Baptists of England, Wales, and Ireland to 1660**, (3 vols., 1971-4), ed. *B.R. White*.

11. The contention of J.C. Davis, that the Ranters existed only 'as a projection of the fears and anxieties' of Interregnum society, has received little support from other scholars. See *J.C.*

Davis, **Fear, Myth, and History: the Ranters and the Historians** (Cambridge, 1986); *G.E. Aylmer*, 'Did the Ranters Exist?' **Past and Present**, no. 117 (Nov. 1987); *C. Hill*, 'Abolishing the Ranters', in **A Nation of Change and Novelty** (1990); and *J.F. McGregor, B. Capp, N. Smith*, and *B.J. Gibbons*, 'Fear, Myth, and Furore', **Past and Present**, no. 140 (Aug. 1993). A small group of perhaps 250 Muggletonians was still in existence at the end of the seventeenth century and the 'last Muggletonian' died in 1979. *C. Hill, B. Reay*, and *W. Lamont*, **The World of the Muggletonians** (1983).

12. *A.G. Matthews*, **Calamy Revised, being a revision of Edmund Calamy's 'Account' of the Ministers and Others Ejected and Silenced, 1660-2** (Oxford, 1934). Matthews's work covers only men ejected from English livings. Men ejected from livings in Wales are studied in *R.T. Jones* and *B.G. Owens*, 'Anghydffurfwyr Cymru, 1660-62', **Y Cofiadur**, xxxii (1962).

13. **The Compton Census of 1676**, ed. *A. Whiteman* (1986).

14. *M. Mullett*, **Sources for the History of English Nonconformity, 1660-1830** (1991), 97.

15. The registrations of Nonconformist meetings for Staffordshire and Wiltshire have been published. *B. Donaldson*, ed., **The Registrations of Dissenting Chapels and Meeting Houses in Staffordshire, 1689-1852**, Staffordshire Record Society, 4th series, iii (1960). *J.H. Chandler*, ed., **Wiltshire Dissenters' Meeting House Certificates and Registrations, 1689-1852** (Devizes, 1985).

16. *A. Brockett*, ed. **The Exeter Assembly. The Minutes of the Assemblies of the United Brethren of Devon and Cornwall, 1691-1717**, Devon and Cornwall Record Society, New Series, vi (1963).

17. *Watts*, **The Dissenters**, i. 491-510.

18. ibid., 496 n.2.

19. *G.S. de Krey*, **A Fractured Society: The Politics in London in the First Age of Party, 1688-1715** (Oxford, 1985). *J.E. Bradley*, **Religion, Revolution, and English Radicalism**, (Cambridge, 1990).

20. *De Krey*, **A Fractured Society** , 21.

21. *Watts*, **The Dissenters** i. 382-393.

22. *M.R. Watts*, **The Dissenters, ii: The Expansion of Evangelical Nonconformity** (Oxford, 1995), 23, 28, 29.

23. DWL MS 38.5-11.

24. *Watts*, **The Dissenters**, ii. 23, 28, 29.

25. *M.R. Watts*, ed., **Religion in Victorian Nottinghamshire: The Religious Census of 1851** (Nottingham, 1988), i. pp.xi-xiii.

26. **Ibid.**, pp.xvi-xx, xxxi-xxxvi. The most detailed evidence on landholding is provided by the material collected under the Tithe Act of 1836 and preserved in the Inland Revenue records at the Public Record Office. *J. Vickers*, 'Methodism and Society in Central Southern England, 1740-1851', Ph.D. thesis (Southampton, 1987), 385.

27. *Watts*, **Religion in Victorian Nottinghamshire**, pp.xv-xvi.

28. *R. Currie*, 'A Micro-Theory of Methodist Growth', **Proceedings of the Wesley Historical Society**, xxxvi (1967), 68.

29. *J. Obelkevich*, **Religion and Rural Society** (Oxford, 1976). *J. Rule*, 'The Labouring Miner in Cornwall', Ph.D.

thesis (Warwick, 1971). *D. Clark, Between Pulpit and Pew* (Cambridge, 1982).

30. *A. Gilbert, **Religion and Industrial Society*** (1976), 66. *B.J. Biggs*, 'Methodism in a Rural Society: North Nottinghamshire, 1740-1851', Ph.D. thesis (Nottingham, 1975), 428-32. *M.A. Smith*, 'Religion in Industrial Society: the case of Oldham and Saddleworth, 1760-1865', D. Phil. thesis (Oxford, 1987), 231, 367. *P. Rycroft*, 'Church, Chapel, and Community in Craven, 1764-1851', DPhil thesis (Oxford, 1988), 208, 221.

31. *Watts*, **The Dissenters**, i. 346-356; ii, 303-27, 597-601. My findings for the early eighteenth century are substantiated by James Bradley's researches on the 1770s and 1780s. **Religion, Revolution, and English Radicalism**, 63-9.

32. *Vickers*, 'Methodism and Society in Central Southern England', 422-3.

33. The list of Nonconformist registers available in the Public Record Office has been published by the List and Index Society, vol. 42 (1969). The Friends House Library in Euston Road, London, contains a digest of the Quaker registers in the PRO with the entries listed conveniently under alphabetical headings.

34. *Watts*, **The Dissenters**, ii. 676-81.

35. *J.L. Vincent*, **Pollbooks: how Victorians Voted** (Cambridge, 1967).

36. **Wesleyan Chronicle**, 1 Dec 1843 - 20 Sept 1844. *R.J. Olney*, **Lincolnshire Politics, 1832-1885** (Oxford, 1973), 60-1. *D. Pretty*, 'Richard Davies and Nonconformist Radicalism in Anglesey, 1837-68', **Welsh History Review**, ix (1978-9), 435. *R. Currie*, **Methodism Divided** (1968), 49.

37. *J.L. Altholz*, **The Religious Press in Britain, 1760-1900** (Westport, Connecticut, 1989), **passim**.

38. Researchers should be warned that the John Rylands Library, Deansgate, is not the same institution as the John Rylands University Library of Manchester, which is two miles away on Oxford Road. It is the Deansgate Library that houses the Methodist Archives.

39. Some of the outstanding university theses which have never been published, at least in full, include *D.G. Evans*, 'The Growth and Development of Organized Religion in the Swansea Valley, 1820-1890', Ph.D. (University of Wales, 1978); *J.J. Hurwich*, 'Nonconformists in Warwickshire, 1660-1720', Ph.D. (Princeton, 1970); *R. Leese*, 'The Impact of Methodism on Black Country Society', Ph.D. (Manchester, 1972); *R.S. Mortimer*, 'Quakerism in Seventeenth-century Bristol', M.A. (Bristol, 1946); *G.A. Weston*, 'The Baptists of North-West England, 1750-1850', Ph.D. (Sheffield, 1969).

40. Membership figures for all the major denominations at national level are collected by *R. Currie, A. Gilbert*, and *L. Horsley* in their valuable **Churches and Churchgoers**, (Oxford, 1977).

41. These figures are derived from *A.D. Gilbert*, 'The Growth and Decline of Nonconformity in England and Wales', DPhil. thesis (Oxford, 1973), 38-9.

42. *C.B. Turner*, 'Revivals and Popular Religion in Victorian and Edwardian Wales', Ph.D. thesis (University of Wales, 1979), 101.

43. Parliamentary Papers, 1910, Cd.5437, vol. xviii.

44. The results of the MARC Europe

surveys were edited by *Peter Brierley* and published under the titles of **Prospects for the Eighties** (1980), **Prospects for Wales** (1983), **Prospects for the Nineties** (1991), and **'Christian' England: What the English Church Census Reveals** (1991).

45. This is the argument in *E.R. Wickham's* pioneering study of Sheffield, **Church and People in an Industrial City** (1957).

46. This is the theme of *R. Gill's* **Myth of the Empty Church** (1993).

47. I give my own interpretation of church decline in **Why did the English stop going to Church?** (Friends of Dr. Williams's Library annual lecture, 1995).

Glossary of terms used in histories of Nonconformity

Anabaptist
Literally, one who baptizes a second time. Used of radical sects on the Continent who rejected infant baptism in the sixteenth century, and because these sects were associated with the extravagances and violence at Münster in 1534-5 the term 'Anabaptist' was later used as a term of abuse to describe Baptists in England.

Antinomianism
The belief that the Christian elected by God is not bound by the moral law. Calvinists were often accused of Antinomianism by their opponents in the seventeenth and eighteenth centuries.

Arianism
The teaching of the fourth-century Alexandrian priest Arius that Christ is inferior to God. Arianism was an important influence on many Presbyterians in the eighteenth century.

Arminianism
The teaching of the sixteenth-century Dutch theologian Jacob Arminius who rejected the Calvinist doctrine of predestination.

Arminian Methodists
Those Methodists who, following the lead of John Wesley, rejected Calvinism. The term was also used of a small group of Methodists in Derby who in 1832 seceded from the Wesleyan Methodists in protest against the 'despotic acts of superintendents'.

Baptists
Nonconformists who believe that the rite of baptism should he administered only to Christian believers.

Bible Christians
Revivalist denomination based largely in Devon and Cornwall, founded in 1815 as a result of William O'Bryan's expulsion from the Wesleyans. The term was also used by a small group of former Swedenborgians in the Manchester area.

Brownists
Followers of the Elizabethan Separatist Robert Browne, one of the earliest advocates of the gathered church.

Calvinism
The teaching of the sixteenth-century French reformer John Calvin that a person's eternal destiny to either enduring happiness or everlasting punishment is predetermined by God's sovereign decrees.

Calvinistic Methodists
Those Methodists, led initially by Howell Harris and Daniel Rowland in Wales and by George Whitefield in England, who subscribed to Calvin's teaching. The Welsh Calvinistic Methodists separated from the Church of England in 1810-11 and in 1933 formed the Presbyterian Church of Wales.

Congregationalists
Nonconformists who believe that the essential unit of church government is the local independent Christian gathered church. Initially the term was used of those Christians who believed that the ideal of the gathered church could be combined with State support for religion (especially in New England), but after Puritan ministers were ejected from the Church of England in 1662 the name Congregationalist came to be used synonymously with the term Independent. The Congregationalists merged

with the Presbyterians in 1972 to form the United Reformed Church.

Evangelical
The belief that every man and woman is destined to spend eternity in hell unless justified by faith, through the personal experience called conversion, in the sacrifice which Christ made at Calvary.

Fifth Monarchists
Men of the 1650s who believed that the Kingdom of Christ was about to be established on earth.

Gathered church
The belief that the only true church is a group of believers gathered in Christ's name 'by a willing covenant made with their God'.

General Baptists
Baptists who believed that salvation was general to all men and women, not particular to the elect.

Independent Methodists
Small denomination founded in 1805-6 by secessionist Methodist groups who rejected a paid ministry.

Independents
Nonconformists who believed in the independence of the local church from superior ecclesiastical authority. The term was used in the 1640s to describe both Separatists from the established church and Congregationalists who believed that the concept of the gathered church could be reconciled with State support for religion.

Methodist Church
Denomination founded in 1932 by the union of the Wesleyan Methodist Church, the Primitive Methodist Connexion, and the United Methodist Church.

Methodist New Connexion
Denomination founded by Alexander Kilham in 1797 to give laymen representation in the annual Conference. Merged with the United Methodist Free Church and the Bible Christians in 1907 to form the United Methodist Church.

New Connexion of General Baptists
Denomination founded in 1770 by Evangelical General Baptists who disliked the growth of liberal theological views among the Old General Baptists. The New Connexion of General Baptists merged with the Particular Baptists in 1891.

Particular Baptists
Calvinistic Baptists who believed that salvation was particular to the elect, not general for all men.

Presbyterians
Calvinists who believed in the parity of ministers in a hierarchy of conferences, synods, and assemblies. Parliament attempted to establish a national Presbyterian Church of England in the 1640s but in 1662 Presbyterian ministers were ejected from their livings and in the course of the eighteenth century many Presbyterian ministers and congregations became Unitarian. Orthodox Presbyterians constituted the Presbyterian Church in England, which was founded in 1839 'in connexion with the Church of Scotland' but which followed the Free Church of Scotland after the disruption of 1843, and the United Presbyterian Church, founded in 1847 as a result of the union of two Scottish dissenting denominations, the United Secession and the Relief churches. In 1876 the Presbyterian Church in England and the United Presbyterians united to form the Presbyterian Church of England, and in 1972 merged with the Congregationalists to constitute the United Reformed Church.

Primitive Methodists
Revivalist denomination formed in 1811 as a result of the Wesleyan Conference's

denunciation of camp meetings. United with the Wesleyans and United Methodists in 1932 to form the Methodist Church.

Protestant Methodists
Denomination founded in 1827 in protest at the decision of the Wesleyan Conference to support the installation of an organ in a Leeds chapel. Later united with the Wesleyan Methodist Association.

Puritans
Protestants who wanted to purge the Church of England of its remaining Catholic elements after the accession of Elizabeth 1. Although the term was initially used of Separatists it was more often used of men who hoped to reform the Church of England from within until they were ejected by the Act of Uniformity of 1662 to become Dissenters.

Quakers
Followers of the seventeenth-century seer George Fox.

Ranters
The name given, in the seventeenth century, to Antinomians who were accused of flouting the moral code and, in the nineteenth century, to the Primitive Methodists.

Separatists
Men and women who, in the reigns of Elizabeth and the early Stuarts, separated from the Church of England to form gathered churches.

Seventh-day Baptists
Baptists who observed the Jewish Sabbath rather than the Christian Sunday as the day of rest and worship.

Society of Friends
Official name of the Quakers.

Socinians
Followers of the sixteenth-century Italian heretic Fausto Sozzini who rejected the doctrines of the Trinity and Christ's vicarious atonement. Many Presbyterians were won over to Socinian ideas in the late eighteenth and nineteenth centuries.

Strict Baptists
Baptists who held High Calvinist views and who insisted on baptism as a condition of communion.

Swedenborgians
Followers of the eighteenth-century Swedish mystic Emanuel Swedenborg who claimed that Christ had returned to earth in 1757 to set up the church of the New Jerusalem.

Unitarians
Christians who rejected the doctrine of the Trinity. While some Socinians claimed that they were the only true Unitarians, Arians also regarded themselves as Unitarians.

United Methodist Church
Denomination formed in 1907 by the union of the United Methodist Free Church, the Methodist New Connexion, and the Bible Christians.

United Methodist Free Church
Denomination formed in 1857 by the union of the Wesleyan Methodist Association and the Wesleyan Reformers.

United Reformed Church
Denomination founded in 1972 by the union of the English Presbyterians and Congregationalists.

Wesleyan Methodist Association
Denomination founded in 1835 in protest at the Wesleyan Conference's decision to set up a theological college.

Wesleyan Methodist Connexion
The organisation established by John Wesley which broke with the Church of England in the 1790s, suffered numerous secessions over the next sixty years, and

reunited with most other Arminian (i.e. non-Calvinistic) Methodists to form the Methodist Church in 1932.

Wesleyan Reformers. Methodists who seceded from the Wesleyan Methodist Connexion in protest at the expulsion, in 1849, of James Everett, Samuel Dunn, and William Griffith in the aftermath of the *Fly Sheets* controversy. Less than half the Wesleyan Reformers joined the Wesleyan Methodist Association in 1857 to constitute the United Methodist Free Churches.

Wesleyan Reform Union. The union of some of those Wesleyan Reformers who refused to join the United Methodist Free Churches in 1857.

Further Reading

The following is a list of secondary sources which will enable the local historian to place the history of his or her Nonconformist communities in their wider historical context. All works were published in London unless stated otherwise.

GENERAL

Bassett, T. M. **The Welsh Baptists** (Swansea, 1977).

Bebbington, D. W. **Evangelicalism in Modern Britain: A History from the 1730s to the 1980s** (1989).

Beckerlegge, O. A. **The United Methodist Free Churches** (1957).

Binfield, C. **So Down to Prayers: Studies in English Nonconformity, 1780-1920** (1977). A series of evocative essays, mainly on Congregationalists.

Bolam, C. G., Goring, J., Short, H.L., and Thomas, R. **The English Presbyterians: From Elizabethan Puritanism to Modern Unitarianism** (1958).

Brown, K.D. **A Social History of the Nonconformist Ministry in England and Wales** (Oxford, 1988).

Currie, R. **Methodism Divided** (1968). Essential for an understanding of Methodist divisions and reunion.

Currie R., Gilbert, A., and Horsley,L. **Churches and Churchgoers: Patterns of Church Growth in the British Isles since 1700** (Oxford, 1977). Indispensable collection of statistics.

Davies, R. E., and Rupp, G. (eds) **A History of the Methodist Church in Great Britain** (4 vols., 1965-88).

Holt, R. V. **The Unitarian Contribution to Social Progress** (1938).

Jones,R.Tudur **Congregationalism in England, 1662-1962** (1962). The best of all the denominational histories.

Jones, R.Tudur **Hanes Annibynwr Cymru** (Abertawe, 1966). History of the Welsh Independents.

Kendall, H. B. **The Origins and History of the Primitive Methodist Church** (2 vols., 1902). A mine of information with lovely photographs.

Parker, G. (ed) **The Centenary of the Methodist New Connexion** (1897).

McLachlan, H. **The Unitarian Movement in the Religious Life of England** (1934).

Mullett, M. **Sources for the History of English Nonconformity, 1660-1830** (1991).

Rees, T. **History of Protestant Nonconformity in Wales** (2nd edn., 1883). After more than a century it has not been superseded.

Rees. T. M. **History of the Quakers in Wales** (Carmarthen, 1925).

Samuelsson, K. **Religion and Economic Action,** translated by G.

French (Stockholm, 1961). The best critique of the Weber thesis.

Sellers, I. **Nineteenth-century Nonconformity** (1977).

Shaw, T. **The Bible Christians, 1815-1907** (1965).

Thompson, D. **Nonconformity in the Nineteenth Century** (1972). Selection of documents with commentary.

Underwood, A.C. **A History of the English Baptists** (1947).

Watts, M.R. **The Dissenters: i, From the Reformation to the French Revolution** (Oxford, 1978).

Watts, M.R. **The Dissenters: ii, The Expansion of Evangelical Nonconformity** (Oxford, 1995).

Weber, M. **The Protestant Ethic and the Spirit of Capitalism,** translated by T. Parsons (1930). The classic, and highly controversial, attempt to explain Nonconformist business success.

Williams, A.H. **Welsh Wesleyan Methodists** (Bangor, 1935).

RADICALS AND PURITANS, 1532-1660

Acheson, R.J. **Radical Puritans in England, 1550-1660** (1990).

Barbour, H. **The Quakers in Puritan England** (New Haven, Conn., 1964).

Braithwaite, W. C. **The Beginnings of Quakerism** (2nd edn., 1955).

Davies, H. **Worship and Theology in England: From Andrewes to Baxter** (1975).

Greaves, R.L. 'The Puritan-Nonconformist Tradition in England, 1560-1700', **Albion,** xvii (Winter, 1985), 449-486. A useful historiographical essay.

Hill, C. **The World Turned Upside Down: Radical Ideas during the English Revolution** (1972). Stimulating study by a leading Marxist historian.

Horst, I.B. **The Radical Brethren** (Niewkoop, 1972).

Jenkins, G. **Protestant Dissenters in Wales, 1639-89** (Cardiff, 1992).

McGregor, J.F., and Reay, B.G. **Radical Religion in the English Revolution** (Oxford, 1984).

Nuttall, G.F. **Visible Saints: the Congregational Way, 1640-1660** (Oxford, 1957).

Peel, A. **The First Congregational Churches** (1920). Anachronistic title of a study of Elizabethan Separatism.

Reay, B.G. **Quakers and the English Revolution** (1985).

Richards, T. **The Puritan Movement in Wales, 1639-53** (1920).

Richards, T. **Religious Developments in Wales, 1654-62** (1923). Both books by Richards are essential for an understanding of the early history of Welsh Nonconformity, but they are very heavy going.

Tolmie, M. **The Triumph of the Saints: the Separate Churches of London, 1616-1649** (Cambridge, 1978).

White, B.R. **The English Separatist Tradition** (Oxford, 1971).

White, B.R. **The English Baptists of the Seventeenth Century** (1983).

PERSECUTION AND TOLERATION, 1660-1730

Braithwaite, W. C. **The Second Period of Quakerism** (2nd edn., 1961).

Brown, R. **The English Baptists of the Eighteenth Century** (1986).

Cragg, G.R. **Puritanism in the Period of the Great Persecution, 1660-88** (Cambridge, 1957). Another book with an anachronistic title, and marred by its failure to distinguish between the various Nonconformist denominations.

Davies, H. **Worship and Theology in England: From Watts and Wesley to Maurice, 1690-1850** (1961).

De Krey, G.S. **A Fractured Society: the Politics of London in the First Age of Party, 1688-1715** (Oxford, 1985).

Greaves, R.L. **Deliver us from Evil: the Radical Underground, 1660-1663.** (Oxford, 1986).

Greaves, R.L. **Enemies under his Feet: Radicals and Nonconformists in Britain, 1664-1677** (Stanford, California, 1990).

Greaves, R.L. **Secrets of the Kingdom: British Radicals from the Popish Plot to the Revolution of 1688-89** (Stanford, California, 1992). The three books by Greaves suggest that the governments of Charles II were justified in their suspicions of the political loyalty and insurrectionary threat posed by some Nonconformists.

Lacey, D. R. **Dissent and Parliamentary Politics in England, 1661-89** (New Brunswick, New Jersey, 1969).

McLachlan, H. **English Education under the Test Acts** (Manchester, 1931). Standard work on the Dissenting academies.

Richards, T. **Wales under the Penal Code** (1925).

Richards, T. **Wales under the Indulgence** (1928).

Vann, R. **The Social Development of English Quakerism, 1655-1755** (Cambridge, Massachusetts, 1969).

Whiting, C. E. **Studies in English Puritanism, 1660-88** (1931). Yet another book with an anachronistic title.

UNITARIANS AND EVANGELICALS, 1730-1851

Bradley, J. **Religion, Revolution, and English Radicalism** (Cambridge, 1990). Important study of the political influence of Nonconformity in the second half of the eighteenth century.

Carwardine, R. **Transatlantic Revivalism: Popular Evangelicalism in Britain and America, 1790-1865** (Westport, Conn., 1978).

Church, L.T, **The Early Methodist People** (2nd. edn., 1949).

Church, L.T. **More About Early Methodist People** (1949).

Davies, E.T. **Religion in the Industrial Revolution in South Wales** (Cardiff, 1965).

Gilbert, A.D. **Religion and Society in Industrial England** (1976). A pioneering statistical study and a stimulating attempt to explain the expansion of Nonconformity.

Gowland, D.A. **Methodist Secessions: The Origins of Free Methodism in Three Lancashire Towns** (Chetham Society, Manchester, 1979). A study of Liverpool, Manchester, and Rochdale.

Harrison, B. **Drink and the Victorians: the Temperance Question in England, 1815-1872** (1971).

Hempton, D. **Methodism and Politics in British Society, 1750-1850** (1984). The non-Wesleyan Methodists and Wales are in fact ignored.

Jones, I. G., and Williams, D. **The Religious Census of 1851: a Calendar of Returns relating to Wales i, South Wales** (Cardiff 1976); **ii, North Wales** (Cardiff 1981). Contains the best introduction to the census.

Jones, R.M. **The Later Periods of Quakerism** (2 vols., 1921).

Laqueur, T.W. **Religion and Respectability: Sunday Schools and Working-class Culture, 1780-1850** (New Haven, Conn., 1976). An important rejoinder to E. P. Thompson.

Lincoln, A. **Some Political and Social Ideas of English Dissent** (Cambridge, 1938).

Lineham, P.J. 'The English Swedenborgians, 1770-1840', DPhil, thesis (Sussex, 1978).

Lovegrove, D.W. **Established Church, Sectarian People: Itinerancy and the Transformation of English Dissent, 1780-1830** (Cambridge, 1988).

Machin, G.I.T. **Politics and the Churches in Great Britain, 1832-1868** (Oxford, 1977).

Roberts, G.M. (ed) **Hanes Methodistiaeth Galfinaidd Cymru** (2 vols., Caernarfon, 1973-8). History of the Welsh Calvinistic Methodists up to 1814.

Rule, J.G. 'The Labouring Miner in Cornwall', Ph.D. thesis (Warwick 1971). Includes an important study of working-class Methodism.

Seed, J. 'The Role of Unitarianism in the Formation of Liberal Culture, 1775-1851 ', Ph.D. thesis (Hull, 1981). Another valuable thesis that has remained largely unpublished, apart from an article in the *Historical Journal, xxviii* (1983), 299-325.

Stigant, E. P. 'Methodism and the Working Class', Ph.D. thesis (Manchester, 1972). A provocative study in the E. P. Thompson tradition, unfortunately unpublished apart from an article in *Northern History,* **vi** (1976).

Thompson, E.P. **The Making of the English Working Class** (1963). Includes a famous diatribe against Methodists by the Marxist son of a Methodist minister.

Ward, W.R. **Religion and Society in England, 1790-1850** (1972). An unduly pessimistic account of the attempts by the churches in general and the Methodists in particular to meet the social and political challenges of the first half of the nineteenth century.

Watts, M.R. **Religion in Victorian Nottinghamshire: the Religious Census of 1851** (2 vols., Nottingham, 1988). An attempt to reinterpret the statistics provided by the religious census and use them to plot the geographic distribution of Dissent at county level.

Wearmouth, R.F. **Methodism and the Common People of the Eighteenth Century** (1945).

Wearmouth, R.E. **Methodism and the Working-class Movements of England, 1800-1850** (1937).

Werner, J.S. **The Primitive Methodist Connexion** (Madison, Wisconsin, 1984). Not only the best account of the origins of Primitive Methodism but also the best account of Wesleyan Methodism in the late eighteenth and early nineteenth centuries.

CRISIS AND CONSCIENCE, FROM 1851

Bebbington, D.W. **The Nonconformist Conscience: Chapel and Politics, 1870-1914** (1982).

Bebbington, D.W. **Victorian Nonconformity** (1992). Introductory essay.

Brake, G.T. **Policy and Politics in British Methodism, 1932-82** (1984).

Briggs, J., and Sellers, I **Victorian Nonconformity** (1973). Collection of documents.

Chadwick, O. **The Victorian Church** (2 vols., 1966-70). Mainly about Anglicans, but contains a sparkling chapter on Nonconformists.

Clark, D. **Between Pulpit and Pew: Folk Religion in a North Yorkshire Village** (Cambridge, 1982). Another important study of popular Methodism.

Cox, J. **The English Churches in a Secular Society: Lambeth, 1870-1930** (Oxford, 1982). A challenging explanation of the decline of religion.

Cunningham, V. **Everywhere Spoken Against: Dissent in the Victorian Novel** (Oxford, 1975). Contains one of the best introductions to Victorian Nonconformity.

Davies, H. **Worship and Theology in England: From Newman to Martineau, 1850-1900** (1962).

Davies, H. **Worship and Theology in England: The Ecumenical Century, 1900-1965** (1965).

Gilbert, A.D. **The Making of Post-Christian Britain** (1980).

Gill, R. **The Myth of the Empty Church** (1993). Argues that a major factor in church decline was competitive church building.

Glover, W.B. **Evangelical Nonconformists and Higher Criticism in the Nineteenth Century** (1954).

Grant, J.W. **Free Churchmanship in England, 1870-1940** (1955).

Inglis, K.S. **Churches and the Working Classes in Victorian England** (1963). A pioneering study, some of whose basic assumptions have been questioned by recent research.

Isichei, E. **The Victorian Quakers** (Oxford, 1970).

Johnson, M.D. **The Dissolution of Dissent, 1850-1918** (New York, 1987). Not as inclusive as its title implies: it is about Congregationalism in general and Mansfield College, Oxford, in particular.

Jordan, E.K.H. **Free Church Unity** (1956).

Koss, S. **Nonconformity in Modern British Politics** (1975).

Lambert, W. **Drink and Sobriety in Victorian Wales** (Cardiff, 1983).

Machin, G.I.T. **Politics and the Churches in Great Britain, 1869-1921** (Oxford, 1987).

McLeod, H. **Class and Religion in the late Victorian City** (1974). Valuable study of London.

McLeod, H. **Religion and the Working Class in Nineteenth-century Britain** (1984).

McLeod, H. **Religion and Irreligion in Victorian England: How Secular was the Working Class?** (1993). Both these pamphlets by McLeod are useful summaries of recent work in the field.

Moore, R. **Pit-men, Preachers and Politics: the Effects of Methodism in a Durham Mining Community** (1974).

Munson, J. **The Nonconformists: in Search of a Lost Culture** (1991). Brilliant evocation of Nonconformity in the generation before the First World War.

Obelkevich, J. **Religion and Rural Society: South Lindsey, 1825-75** (Oxford, 1976). The best study of rural Methodism.

Parsons, G. (ed) **Religion in Victorian Britain** (4 vols., Manchester, 1988).

Sandall, R., and Wiggins, A.R. **The History of the Salvation Army** (4 vols., 1947-64).

Scotland, N. **Methodism and the Revolt of the Field** (Gloucester, 1981).

Turner, C.B. 'Revivals and Popular Religion in Victorian and Edwardian Wales', Ph.D. thesis (University of Wales, 1979). The best treatment of the subject and again unpublished.

Watts, M.R. **Why did the English stop going to church?** (1995).